Of Birds and Words

Susan Bass Marcus

© 2025 Susan Bass Marcus

All rights reserved. No part of this publication may be reproduced, distributed, or transmitted in any form or by any means, including photocopying, recording, or other electronic or mechanical methods, without the prior written permission of the publisher, except in the case of brief quotations embodied in critical reviews and certain other non commercial uses permitted by copyright law.

This is a work of fiction. All the names, characters, and places in this book are the product of the author's imagination. Any resemblance to actual persons, living or dead, or actual events is purely coincidental.

Paperback ISBN: 978-1-7321434-7-0

Ebook ISBN: 978-1-7321434-8-7

Book design by Sarah E. Holroyd

       (https://sleepingcatbooks.com)

Cover artwork by Susan Bass Marcus

To Stephen, who shares our love for birds

Preface

"What kind of bird is that?"

"A sparrow, a robin?"

"A . . . actually, I don't know."

My husband and I let it pass. Then came the 2020 pandemic, and our long morning walks began. Caught up in our work, our obligations, and a gym membership, we had taken few walks through our neighborhood, and so much of it was unfamiliar.

COVID-19 changed our daily routine. By March–and still healthy–we were exploring quiet lakeside park paths unpopulated by other walkers. As we strode along, and in the absence of other people, we discovered urban life we'd never noticed before. Skeletal winter trees looking stark, punching their outlines against the grey winter sky. Hibernating, but full of spring promise. Foxes stalking crows in Chicago's Maggie Daley Park. A red-tailed hawk feasting on a pigeon. Even two deer grazing in a park above the Metra tracks downtown.

Choruses of bird song caught our attention–a great variety of unknown birds. We started a list of those we identified and ultimately treasured: cardinals and crows, sparrows and finches, hairy and downy woodpeckers, dark-eyed juncos, rock pigeons, mourning doves, dickcissels, thrushes, ducks (both mallard and merganser), killdeer, an American woodcock, and so many more.

Months later, after sketching a few of our sightings, I began to draw imaginary birds, goofy birds, spoofy birds, until I amassed a folder filled with drawings. After I described my drawings to my online writers' group friends, they suggested that I create a book about them. I liked the idea.

I redrew most of the sketches and punched up their vibrancy. I created a taxonomy for the collection–having given the birds invented common names, I classified each one with a Latin-ish genus and species. And yet, who were these birds? As you will see, a poem, anecdote, or fable tells some aspect of each bird's story.

Have fun with my avian friends. At the end of this little book, you will meet the dearest of my characters, whose love of birds reflects my own. Up, up, and away!

Acknowledgements

With many thanks for the support of my friends and fellow writers, Jan, Brian, my editor and book designer Sarah Holroyd, and fellow members of our Chicago writers' group. I am deeply grateful for the wisdom, critiques, and enthusiasm of Stephen Marcus, my husband.

Contents

Preface	v
Acknowledgements	vii
Reader Owl and Owlet (*Bubo lector*)	2
Chicken Little (*Gallus parum*)	4
Bluishbird and Fancydress Goose (*Avis caeruleus et Anser ornatus*)	6
Clown Birds (*Aves scurrae*)	8
Artichoke Bird (*Avis cynara*)	10
Chef Bird and Mouse (*Avis coquus*) and (*Mus*)	12
Chick and worm (*Avis pullus*) and (*Vermis pomonella*)	14
Uncommon Anteater Bird (*Avis rara formicafagensis*)	16
Too-Late Bird (*Avis nimis-serus*)	18
The Golden Irate (*Avis irata aurea*)	20
Dancing Crane (*Gruis saltatens*)	22
Yellow-bellied Maxibill (*Avis sadsaquus*)	24
Buff Orange Comet (*Gallus balatro*)	26
Iterant Clad Cuckoo (*Cuculus vagus*)	28
Yellow Raincatcher (*Passer pluviophile*)	30
Cocoa Snowcatcher (*Passer frigendus*)	32
Wintering Spadger (*Passer hiemandi frigoris*)	34
Blue-Headed Lovebird (*Agapornis rara*)	36
Red-Breasted Phoebegale (*Passer quae elige*)	38
Crested Daytripper (*Avis viator perdiem*)	40
Bird of Heaven and Batbird (*Avis decaelis*) and (*Avis verspertilio*)	42

Regalia Penguin and Chick (*Pinguinus indutusest*)	44
Pan's Apprentice and Rocker's Wren (*Troglodytes melicus*)	46
Uncommon Tern (*Sterna rara*)	48
Uncommon Tern (*Sterna rara cocta*)	50
Uncommon Tern (*Sterna rara mea-non-tua*)	52
Uncommon Tern (*Sterna rara vermivora*)	54
Uncommon Tern (*Sterna rara in angulara*)	56
Uncommon Tern (*Sterna rara angulara*)	58
Uncommon Tern (*Sterna rara*)	60
Uncommon Tern (*Sterna rara*)	62
Uncommon Tern (*Sterna rara*)	64
Uncommon Tern (*Sterna rara piscator*)	66
Uncommon Tern (*Sterna rara*)	68
Minor Marvelbird (*Avis admirari*)	70
Faculty Bird (*Avis academicus*)	72
Grumpy's Bird (*Avis malevolum*)	74
Hatcher's Hairy Heron (*Ardea pilosa*)	76
Dragon Bird (*Avis draconis*)	78
Gerty Bird (*Avis gertya*)	80
Lexicon	82
Author Bio	85
Also by Susan Bass Marcus	86

Reader Owl and Owlet (*Bubo lector*)

"Dad" and "Owlet"

It was late, nearly morning. Owlet paced the branch. Every so often, he glanced at his father, poked his tail feathers, and squeaked. Nothing could tear his father's eyes from the pages of the book he was reading. Each story outdid the last in scary or surreal details. Owlet noticed the title.

Reader Owl sneezed and looked up. "This book is such a hoot."

"Dad, you promised to teach me how to hunt mice tonight. You're still reading. That's *your* wrong move."

"No, the title is *The Wrong Move and Other Stories*, but well done, my son. You read at least some of it. Mother will be so proud."

"But Dad . . ."

"Just a few more pages, my dear child. We shall have adventures soon. We'll fly above the forest wild. On silent wings and under the moon."

"That's a lovely bit of verse, Dad, but the sun's coming up."

"Just this last short story, my boy, and I promise that we'll hunt."

Owlet's ears perked up. "Never mind. I hear something." He flew over the forest floor below. On swooping wings, he snatched a scurrying mouse.

Reader Owl closed the book. "Son, where are you? Ah, I see you have made the right move. I knew you could do it on your own."

Owlet spit out a pellet of mouse bones. "Thanks, Dad. I just needed a push."

Chicken Little (*Gallus parum*)

(A Haiku)

"The sky is falling!"

I shouted so many times

Nobody listened

                ***

I paced 'round the yard

While scanning the sky above

Acorns hit my head

("Oh, I see. Sorry.")

Bluishbird and Fancydress Goose
(*Avis caeruleus et Anser ornatus*)

"Barry" and "Gladys"

Barry arrived with a gilt-edged invitation to the Annual Avian Fancy Ball.

Gladys was delighted and said, "I'd love to go, but I haven't a thing to wear."

"No worries, my dear," he assured her. "Just come as you dare."

She: "In this old thing, that skirt, this hat?"

He: "You are the image of an aristocrat."

She: "Well, I accept your kind request,

because you think I'll look my best."

He extended his wing

And she offered one too.

Their legs then did spring

As up, up they flew.

Barry and Gladys,

Dressed up for the ball,

Soaring straight westward

Entranced with it all.

Clown Birds (*Aves scurrae*)

"Vladimir" and "Tarragon"*

On stage, at the [tree branch] crossroads, two clown birds sit.

They are waiting for someone or something.*

"We have to go, Vlad, or the circus will leave without us."

"Tarragon, struggle is futile. The essential doesn't change. He will come."

"Well, he is late. We shall lose our jobs. What will you ask?"

"Um, nothing precisely."

"A vague supplication for . . . ?"

"Time."

"Well, I would ask for something else."

"Like?"

Tarragon sighs. "A raise."

Nothing else happens.

The stage lights dim.

(*Thanks to Samuel Beckett and *Waiting for Godot*)

Artichoke Bird (*Avis cynara*)

"Archie"

(A Haiku)

I'm good with butter

But do not tear me apart

You will break my heart

              ***

I may be thorny

You'll choke on my heart for I

Once was a woman.

–oh, that Zeus!*

Myth: *Kynara, a nymph, angered the Greek god Zeus,

and he turned her into an artichoke. Beware of multiple puns.

Chef Bird and Mouse (*Avis coquus*) and (*Mus*)

"Tito" and "Mike"

Tito: "I can't let you take that. It's for the hen party."

Mike: "Sorry. What else do you have?"

Tito: "Steel-cut oats?"

Mike: "Too sharp."

Tito: "Celery?"

Mike: "Stringy."

Tito: "Cucumbers?"

Mike: "Watery."

Tito: "Well, that beats all."

Mike: "Beets? Perfect. What do I owe you?"

Tito: "Cashews?"

Mike: "Gesundheit."

Chick and worm (*Avis pullus*) and (*Vermis pomonella*)

"Joe" and "Worm"

A chick flew into an orchard far ahead of his flock. He saw an apple on the ground. A worm emerged from a hole near the apple's stem. The chick cocked his head as the worm wiggled up. The worm said, "You're far too early, kid."

Unnerved by the worm's nervy put-down, the chick wandered around the farm until he saw a barn. There, he met an old, whiskery pig who introduced himself as Wilbur. "Mr. Wilbur," said the chick, "my name is Joe. What is your secret to a long life? Most pigs end up as bacon and ham early on."

Wilbur said, "Find and befriend one of the spiders living here. They don't live long but they like to have a purpose in life." Wilbur grunted goodbye and waddled out of the barn.

After scratching the barnyard dirt for mites and small beetles with little success, Joe approached some barn spiders and asked to be their friend. No one answered him. Joe bent his little legs and sank to the barn's hay-bristly floor. "Poor me. No worm will ever let me be the early bird that catches him, no matter how hard I try to arrive at just the right moment. What can I do?"

"Ah-hem," he heard behind his tail feathers. "I can help you, little fellow." Joe looked at the cow stall behind him and saw a large orb weaver, yellow and brown with eight striped legs.

"Wow! How beautiful you are! Your web, too," peeped Joe. "I would never eat one as lovely as you. I want to eat worms. Trouble is, they always laugh at me. My name is Joe. What is yours?"

"My name is Simone. I have an idea, something I heard Wilbur say. Sleep here until morning. I think you'll like what you'll see."

Joe roosted on a beam under the barn's roof just as the cows were returning from pasture. The farmer came to milk the cows, then left and closed the barn door.

The next morning as the sun was peeping over the hills, Joe woke up. The barn door was open, and the cows were on their way to graze. Joe flew from his perch through a window and into the orchard. He hopped to a half-crushed apple that had fallen from a tree. A worm was poking its head out of the apple. It looked at Joe and cried, "Oh, please, little chick, eat me, eat me right now." What a surprise! Nevertheless, Joe obliged. The worm was delicious.

Puzzled, he flew back to the open barn door, which was now cloaked with an enormous web heavy with dew. Joe saw shapes running across the web's concentric circles. Just then, the farmer strode by and stopped. "Well, I'll be," he said. "Who knew I had a famous chick here?" Out loud, he read the web's design: "Some Chick," "Feed Him," "Be Famous."

Joe mused, "I didn't know worms could read." (Thanks to E.B. White and *Charlotte's Web*)

Uncommon Anteater Bird (*Avis rara formicafagensis*)

"UAB"

With her long tongue and hard bill ready, this Uncommon Anteater Bird has spotted her next meal.

Having lost their queen, nearly 1,000 ants are moving from their disintegrating hill to a new home.

Dressed in her fanciest short trousers, UAB is feasting on the parade.

When asked about the ants' flavor, she replies, "A bit tangy and woody, like pencil shavings, with a mineral finish."

One little fellow has escaped her hungry eye.

Too-Late Bird (*Avis nimis-serus*)

"Trish"

Like American goldfinches, the too-late bird nests later than most songbirds. In fact, if the early bird (*Avis primitus*) always gets the worm, the too-late bird consistently misses the season and must find alternative nutrition. Fortunately, she is chic and aware of current fashion trends. These assets draw attention and provide her with bountiful handouts until she settles into nesting. From then on, her less noticeable mate provides for them both. When asked if she misses the taste of worms, she denies ever liking them and insists on her preference for caviar.

The Golden Irate (*Avis irata aurea*)

"Tinnitus"

This old bird was once a jolly, mischievous chick always ready to steal a beetle from his fellow nestlings or prank his friends.

However, his species transforms dramatically when a fledgling becomes an adult.

The mature golden irate loses his sense of humor. He prefers solitude and has zero tolerance for young (and in his mind "frivolous") goldens. Hence, when an impertinent chick approaches, Tinnitus hunches his wings, lowers his beak, and sings, "Humph, kids today," which sounds like a burst of bus exhaust.

Dancing Crane (*Gruis saltatens*)

"Tippy"

With a graceful jeté and pointed left toes, Tippy the dancing crane welcomes spring as she waits for her mate to come courting again. She is dressed in her brightest seasonal outfit, which complements her stunning blue plumage. As the days lengthen, the cranes' annual ballet will confirm their life-long commitment. Observers have noted that they also dance throughout the year, whenever the spirit moves them.

If they can avoid disease or predators, this couple will live up to 20 years. They can look forward to lots of jumping for joy as they choreograph expressions of their devotion.

But what of their offspring? When do their babies, called "colts," learn their first ballroom steps? Young but precocious, they start practicing at two months! They often join their parents during their first year as they twirl and frolic. All that dancing triggers gradual molting, and in their second year, their plumage matches their parents' azure hue. At the end of their second year, they reach maturity. When they find a suitable partner, they leap into their own courting dance.

Yellow-bellied Maxibill (*Avis sadsaquus*)

"Twixt"

Distantly related to storks and herons, Twixt the maxibill lives exclusively on a small Pacific Ocean island, the name of which remains undisclosed to protect this rare species from extinction. Not to be confused with similar-looking gigantic terror birds that existed 50 million years ago, the maxibill eats only plants. It lives symbiotically with the equally rare giant pink vermes, a large worm that burrows into the island's soil. The worm's activity encourages plant growth, the basis of Twixt's diet. The pink vermes's diet consists mainly of the bird's waste. Together they contribute to the island's balanced nature.

Twixt is not an active creature. Content to munch on green leaves, he spends his days grazing and resting in the shade of palm trees, the identity of which remains secret–again, in order to save the island's inhabitants from extinction. Over millennia, the maxibill has been living quietly and has developed a characteristic yellow paunch, which its mate finds highly attractive. As long as the bird's habitat remains unchallenged by tourism, climate change, and invasive species, cryptozoologists feel assured that studies of this unusual bird will continue to reveal many of nature's most astounding secrets.

Buff Orange Comet (*Gallus balatro*)

"Incognito"

This rooster belongs to a bantam breed of comets akin to Nankin fancy chickens, with which he lives as flock jester. Normally calm with a likeable personality, the buff orange comet sticks very close to his flock and rarely ventures far. Seasonally, however, he becomes animated and highly sociable.

The comet has never revealed his hatchling name. The Nankins tease him with the sobriquet "Party Poultry," or "Pulcinello," because this rooster tends to dress up in fall colors, especially burnt orange. In his most active season, he ranges freely in the barnyard while surveying the flock's hens. On days when he sports his finest yellow jacket and orange boots, the comet circles his target hen at high speed while serenading her with an appropriate operatic aria.

As soon as he crows–his doodle-doo is always off key–the hen attracting his attention cackles long and loudly as she rolls in the yard's gravel and kicks her feet in the air.

With his beak pressed into the top button of his jacket, the buff orange comet then exiles himself to a fence post and spends the rest of the day in a sulk. Nevertheless, until the season passes, he will pursue his chosen hen with the hope that one day she will stop cackling and will give him a coo.

Iterant Clad Cuckoo (*Cuculus vagus*)

"Treble"

Known for its distinctive call, the iterant clad cuckoo distinguishes itself from common cuckoos by breaking with tradition. One day, while serving as principal singer in the bell tower of a clock in Prague, Czech Republic, Treble stood on the clock's platform and sang out an extra note. Passersby and tourists expecting the usual two-note version of the hourly announcement were all shocked at this departure from custom.

Complaints rained on the keeper of the clock. He climbed to the tower's roof. Interrupting Treble's midday meal, the keeper reminded him that clock cuckoos are obligated to sing only two notes on the hour. Any deviation is cause for dismissal. With that, the keeper ordered him to vacate the tower by morning's first light.

Regretting his impulsive and surprising behavior, Treble the iterant clad cuckoo buttoned up his yellow jacket, stuffed his pockets with extra seeds, and left Prague. He flew for weeks across Europe, over Iceland, past the New England states, until he landed in Iowa.

Ames, Iowa, to be precise, where the local weather station hired him as a weathervane. Proudly wearing a station beanie topped by a rotating propeller, Treble now works as a tornado spotter and general weather prognosticator. The new job pleases him immensely because his song includes more than three notes and the station director loves them all.

Yellow Raincatcher (*Passer pluviophile*)

"Tilda"

After a long, hellish drought, after hopping days on end over dry, flattened grasses, after pecking fruitlessly at cracked earth for seeds and bugs, Tilda the yellow raincatcher lifted her beak and sang for joy. At last, rain was falling.

As her name suggests, this species of sparrow loves rain. For days, the land swallowed rainwater until it could hold no more. Puddles grew into shallow ponds. Splashing at the edge of a pond Tilda sang and sang.

The rain passed. Too soon, the dry, drought-plagued times returned. Hungry and drained by another endless search for food, Tilda flew on weary wings to a tree branch. She tucked her beak into her wing feathers and dozed.

She woke with a shiver. A chill wind was shaking her branch. Clinging with her perching feet, she swayed as the tree bent with a brewing storm's fitful gusts. Her eyes widened; she felt an icy drop wet her head. Rain! She opened her beak to catch a drop. Faster and faster the rain fell. The wind blew sheets of rain through the tree. Red and orange leaves flew to the ground.

Tilda fluttered to the tree's base and leaned against its trunk. A puddle was spreading at her feet. She dipped one foot into it, then both feet. She splashed about and flapped her wings.

The wild wind eased at sunset, and Tilda drank from her puddle. She sang and dipped her wings in the wet. Heaven was hers again. Tomorrow she would find seeds and bugs and she would dance in rain puddles.

Cocoa Snowcatcher (*Passer frigendus*)

"Tizzy"

Tizzy the cocoa snowcatcher expected to see the usual icy grey ball that always hung in the sky whenever cold winds dumped snow on his home roost. That morning, as a few clouds drifted past, a glowing orange and yellow ball rose in the sky. Tizzy scanned the sky for clouds signaling his grey ball's return.

Tizzy's heart beat faster as he felt cold winds ruffling his feathers. Those winds always brought snow. He loved the snow. He looked up. No snow. Worse–he felt warm. He did not want to feel warm. He wanted to play in the snow. His spirits sank as he feared he would never see snow again.

Strands of mist drifted overhead. They darkened into clouds. They grew heavy and dropped lower. The cocoa snowcatcher's hopes returned as clouds covered the yellow ball. Wind ruffled his neck feathers, and he shivered. *That was more like it.*

The clouds parted, and the yellow ball reappeared wrapped in haze. It wore a red cap, which surprised Tizzy. He had never seen that before. The yellow ball smiled as heavy clouds gathered around it.

Snowflakes began to fall–big, lazy flakes. They landed on Tizzy's roost and on the buildings around him. More flakes fell and quickly piled up. The world around Tizzy was turning white.

Now, Tizzy the cocoa snowcatcher felt at home, even under that yellow ball in the sky. He thought, "I must never lose hope."

Wintering Spadger (*Passer hiemandi frigoris*)

"Tristan" and "Isolde"

A cold wind buffeted two spadgers perched on twin oak branches. Shivering within her fluffed-up feathers, the female, Isolde, tapped her mate's beak. "I am serious, Tristan, my love. I ask you, why are we still here when the finches, the linnets, and even the cocoa snowcatchers have left for warmer climes?"

Tristan replied, "True. They have left us, just as our children have done."

"On their way to South America. How could they flout tradition so egregiously? And yet..."

"And yet?"

She sang an aria her mate had never heard before. "Oh, to be warm again!"

Tristan groomed his wing feathers. He took a while to scratch them with his toes and preen them with his beak. "Actually, I heard the linnets discuss their plans, and South America was not their destination. They mentioned a place not too far from here, where winters have been warmer than ever before. As they conversed, they rehearsed directions to the place, and I do recall them now."

"Really? Well, I never... would you consider going there with me? Would you remember our way back to this tree in the spring?"

He puffed his breast feathers. "Most assuredly. Shall we go now?"

Isolde bobbed her head. "Let's go! To a warm nest and better food." And off they flew.

Blue-Headed Lovebird (*Agapornis rara*)

Tombo: "Marry me?"

Tiara: "I'll think about it. Give me time.

Right now, I have a taste for lime,

Or figs and seeds, grass or bugs."

Tombo: "I'd be happy with just some hugs

Since I've asked you several times

In song and in fine verse that rhymes."

Tiara: "I'm only teasing. Can't you see?

There's nowhere else I'd rather be

Than by your side in any weather,

Time, or space–we'll be together."

Tombo: "You've made my day, my year, my life.

From this hour on you'll be my wife."

Tiara: "Did I say that? I must amend.

I meant to say, *I'll be your friend.*"

Red-Breasted Phoebegale (*Passer quae elige*)

Mrs. Phoebegale had insisted on migrating to Florida for the winter instead of Mexico. "You will love it, my dear. Warmth, insects, a peaceful, wild place with no cars and few people." Doubting the reliability of her enthusiastic description, Mr. Phoebegale nevertheless agreed to the change in plans. They ate as many beetles and seeds as possible and, with plenty of nourishment stored in their fat, they left Chicago.

The flight south was long, and conditions varied. They landed on Amelia Island, together with migrating cedar waxwings, indigo buntings, and snowy owls. The saltmarsh estuaries were comfortable, food was abundant, and they considered staying for the season.

But there were pebbles in the bird seed, so to speak. River otters and alligators began to stalk them in that false paradise. Mr. P. barely escaped the talons of a bald eagle. He flew to a thick clump of palms and sulked the rest of the day.

Although mated for life, Mr. P. was considerably older than Mrs. P. He tired easily. He hated abrupt temperature changes, hurricanes, and predators. His old bones craved safety; his eyes ached in the glare of sunlight.

Mrs. P. was sorry for her mate and to cheer him she sang about everything–a cache of seeds or insects, a shaft of sunlight warming her wings, new friends, or a fine branch for roosting.

One day, Mr. P. announced he no longer could bear the place. Mrs. P. looked sad for a moment, but lifted her beak and said, "I'm happy to leave." They fed furiously for a while then left the warm salt marsh on heavy wings.

As they flew southwest, Mr. P. called to his mate: "Mrs. P., I know you liked Florida, but we could not stay in that nest of perils. Mexico is where we belong."

"No need to explain, my love. I look forward to seeing old friends and feasting on ground beetles, safflower seeds, and aquatic bird fly eggs. I confess, I was afraid of those alligators. Always between us and a good snack. And that eagle–well!" She clicked her beak in agitation. Mr. P. grunted and flew ahead.

They landed in the grasslands of Chihuahua and rushed to greet neighbors from past seasons. They set up their roost and foraged for food. After gobbling grasshoppers, crickets, beetles, wild berries and seeds, cactus fruit, and sunflowers, they settled in.

"Mr. P," said Mrs. P., "I am so happy to be here that I just have to sing about it." She perched on the top pad of a prickly pear cactus and sang, "It's so good to be here in Chihuahua. Florida was nice, but this is better." She flew back to Mr. P.'s side, and there they slept for the rest of the night.

Crested Daytripper (*Avis viator perdiem*)

Louis is happy to be alive.

He just completed trip No. 5.

While migrating south to his old winter stop

He entered a boutique where he liked to shop.

High on a shelf sat a little red basket,

That he longed to wear with his azury outfit.

"How much is that basket?" he asked the owner.

"It's not for sale," she squawked with a glower.

"I'll pay you anything, ma'am, I must have it."

Louis flew to the shelf and suddenly grabbed it.

Dropping his payment as he flew out the door,

The owner behind him, the flock in uproar.

Louis escaped as he flew ever faster.

That little adventure a near-miss disaster.

Alone on a branch of his favorite tree

He called *cheery-bee*, I'm glad to be me.

Bird of Heaven and Batbird (*Avis decaelis*) and (*Avis verspertilio*)

(A Haiku)

Bird of Heaven's song

Does not last long but rises

To celestial heights

***

Batbird's wings are strong

Its song is a gentle peep

As it soars aloft

***

Over towns and farms

Like ships passing in the night

Blind to each other

Regalia Penguin and Chick (*Pinguinus indutusest*)

The regalia penguin and his daughter were on an ice floe heading to a penguin party. Father squawked, "Taxi!" to speed it up, but the floe continued at a dead-fish pace.

"Papa, if this floe doesn't move faster, we are going to be late."

"Patience, daughter," he said. "If I squawk 'Taxi' loudly, it will pick up speed. It's just having one of its moods."

She frowned at her father and said, "I have never heard of a pouting plate of ice."

"You're young. It's a known fact. Ice floes can be like that."

"I didn't know, and–ah-hem–we aren't moving."

Just then, another floe rushed by them with three fastidia penguins on board, all squawking "Taxi, Taxi" as they waved to the regalia and his chick. The young penguin watched them pass by, then turned to her father. "They're leaving us behind. At least they could have offered us a ride." She paused. "Perhaps you did not read all the floe instructions, Papa? The fastidias squawked 'taxi' twice not once."

He beamed at her and flapped his wings. "Ah-ha, my brilliant child. Correct! I did not read past page one." He lifted his beak and screeched, "Taxi! Taxi!"

The floe lurched ahead and sailed so quickly toward the mainland that it passed the other floe. Father and daughter waved to the fastidias and flapped their wings in contentment. "It's going to be a wonderful day," said the daughter. "Taxi! Taxi!" her father continued to squawk and happily nodded his beak.

Pan's Apprentice and Rocker's Wren (*Troglodytes melicus*)

"Peepit"

On a warm, sunny day long, long ago, a little brown wren with a yellow breast and bright blue crest needed help. He was terribly lonely. Whenever he sang his social song, "Let's-Get-Together," no wren accepted his invitation. His territory song, his full-tummy chant, and his morning and evening arias required no response, but he decided it was time to change his social song.

On this day, as the wren flew over a meadow, he came upon a young faun, Pan's apprentice. The wren heard him playing on his pipes. It sounded like wind playing with icicles. Then he spotted the faun sitting on a toadstool.

The wren landed at his feet. He thought, *Perhaps this musician might help me*. Looking up at the chubby young creature, he said, "Hello, my name is Peepit. What's yours?"

"They call me Silvanus," the apprentice said after finishing his piece. He lowered his pipes and stared at the wren. "What can I do for you, Peepit?"

"Silvanus–that's a nice name. I heard your pretty song. Would you please teach me a new one that will attract other wrens? No one answers my social song, and I am so lonely."

"I like being alone," said Silvanus, "but I understand you birds are different." He scratched his rosy cheek and tapped his pipes. "I have an idea. Wrens in my part of the forest sing something like this." And he played a sweet, short melody. "What do you think?"

"I like it very much. Would my wrens like it, too?"

"Indeed! I'll teach it to you. It's called 'Let's Sing Together.'" He played it again and again until Peepit finally learned it as the sun was setting. "Now, return to your roost, little one, and sing it loud and long."

Peepit thanked the young faun and flew back to his favorite branch. Once perched securely, he sang his new song over and over. To his delight a chorus of wren song answered his call. Soon, a small flock of rocker's wrens landed on nearby branches and introduced themselves. They had recognized the song and invited Peepit to join them. He thought, *Oh my goodness. All this time I have been singing some other bird's song. Thank you, Silvanus.*

Uncommon Tern (*Sterna rara*)

"Ted"

(A Haiku)

On his way to play

volleyball on a bright day

Ted, a confused tern,

lost his way and checked

on his mobile for the route

and he realized

that he was lost, so

he made a U-turn *tout de suite*

and arrived on time.

Uncommon Tern (*Sterna rara cocta*)

"Thalia"

Obituary

The last living legend of piscine cuisine, Thalia Sterna, passed away in the kitchen of her own fishbar on the shores of Lake Woeissimie on October 31, 2008. Colleagues reluctantly bowed to her dying wish that she be stewed and served to the community in a ragout of seafood and salt water.

All those attending her memorial service and reception felt that Thalia thereafter was very much a part of their lives and they complimented the fishbar staff on their expert preparation of the ragout.

Sterna leaves countless broods of uncommon tern offspring, including her 10 sons and 14 daughters, to carry her memory forward as an inspiration to future generations.

Uncommon Tern (*Sterna rara mea-non-tua*)

(A Haiku-ish)

"That's my tern," he said

with his wing behind her head.

The other claimed then,

"No, she's mine," he said.

"Excuse me, both of you err,"

She said, "I'm neither

of yours, so there."

Uncommon Tern (*Sterna rara vermivora*)

"Tilly"

[As The Tern Worms]

PISCINE PRESS–Today, Tilly Sterna broke up the happy home of Arthur and Annabelle Annelid. Yesterday evening, a massive thunderstorm moistened the soil and signaled to the couple that they would have an easy migration to their second home across the lawn.

Tilly is a well-known vermivore in the area. She prefers diving after small fish she spots as she flies low over water, but as an uncommon tern she likes to vary her diet with worms and insects, and in winter she wouldn't refuse some dead fish left behind by fishermen.

Witnesses claim that Tilly must have analyzed conditions because she appeared to be waiting for the Annelids. As Arthur began to wiggle through the grass, she swooped in, caught him by the neck, and escaped to the shore. Mrs. Annelid expressed her outrage. "What am I supposed to do now?" Betsy Beetle, standing nearby, advised her to retreat to her hole in case Tilly was still hungry, which Annabelle did, vowing to return after dark.

Uncommon Tern (*Sterna rara in angulara*)

"Trent"

[Idiom: *To tern a corner*]

Trent found work in the city after years of fruitless searches for employment along the shore. It wasn't much. Every day, after lunch, he had to peek around the corner of City Hall. Oscar, an assistant to the mayor, had hired him.

Trent's job grew out of a misunderstanding, but it stayed on the books because no one wanted to appear inept. The mayor had announced to his staff that at last they had turned a corner on solving City Hall's sidewalk issue. A tree root had raised a stretch of the sidewalk and people were tripping over it. The mayor insisted that the staff keep an eye on it. "Let's make it a proper turn of the corner," the mayor exclaimed with a wink.

Oscar–an enthusiastic bird lover–thought that the mayor wanted a tern to keep an eye on the sidewalk. Soon after the meeting, as Oscar was scanning the beach through his binoculars, he spotted Trent. Using a small herring, he enticed the tern to come closer. Trent slurped up the fish and listened to the assistant's job offer. "Sounds good to me," he said, "but what's the pay?"

"A daily basket of fish. You report this afternoon. At the corner of Main and Second Avenue."

"Accepted. You can count on me."

That is why every day on the corner of Main and Second Avenue, at two o'clock in the afternoon you can see Trent peeking around the corner of City Hall.

Uncommon Tern (*Sterna rara angulara*)

"Trent"

After a few years of stellar service to City Hall, Trent lost his job as a sidewalk superintendent and forfeited his bounty of fish. The mayor's staff finally had agreed on the most effective way of resolving the raised sidewalk problem. They removed the aggressive tree that lifted the sidewalk as its roots pushed through the soil. Trent's job became redundant. Oscar, the mayor's assistant and by now a close friend of Trent's, had the sad task of firing his bird friend.

"Don't despair, my old pal," said Oscar. "Your work was remarkable, as was your discretion. I am going to nominate you for first place in a competition just for your kind of bird." Trent appreciated the gesture, but he began to make plans for his return to the shore and a new job search.

Oscar persisted. Trent's record so awed the competition's panel of judges that they agreed unanimously to award Trent first place. A month later, they bestowed on him the highest award any bird in his species could win, Tern of the Century. From that time on, job offers poured in, and Trent spent the rest of his life fully employed and fully fed.

Uncommon Tern (*Sterna rara*)

"Tom"

After spending the early years of his life as a rounder and a cad, Tom decided to change his ways: He would give up fish bars (fermented fish made him stagger and behave badly) and playing the field. A new Tom would fly right and find a mate. His beloved top hat would have to go. It signaled a frivolous nature, and he wanted to be a serious bird, responsible and trustworthy. He would ditch the green tie, too. It made him look silly, hardly a good candidate for a lifelong commitment.

After one last visit to Crabby's, his favorite fish bar, Tom stumbled over a big green leaf. He fell flat on his beak. "What have I done? Could this be a sign? Shall I make a new start right now?" he trilled. "Yes!" He threw his hat and tie into the air, and the sea winds swept them away over the water. "There they go, symbols of my dissolute life. Now, I am re-terning," he shouted to no one in particular. "Terning," he looked down. "Terning over a new leaf."

Well, he tried. It's hard teaching an old tern new flight plans.

Uncommon Tern (*Sterna rara*)

"Tad"

[A "Tern" of Events]

An old unemployed tern named Tad

whose hearing and eyesight were bad,

thought he looked quite his best

in his black velvet vest.

Yet, without work he always felt sad.

One day he had lunch with a friend

who said that this sadness must end.

"I have the right job for you.

It pays a fish pail or two

and you'll work as the Tern of Events."

"Thank you, old pal," Tad did say.

"I'll be happy to start work today."

The friend nodded twice.

He said that was nice,

and old Tad had a really good day.

Uncommon Tern (*Sterna rara*)

"Tilly" and "Theo"

"It's *terning* colder (for now)."

Tilly loves Theo's new boots. "I am happy to see you are dressed properly. The wind won't feel so cold with that scarf around your neck. You'll be grateful for those boots, too."

"Why?" Theo asks.

"To slog through puddles."

Theo blinks and says, "I confess, your scarf and boots say, '*très chic*.'* I wanted that look for myself; and I found both items at the Polar Emporium–on sale! Uh, you said, 'slog through puddles'–what puddles?"

"When the glaciers melt and the floes disappear we will see vast, boundless puddles."

"Oh, my dear, surely by then fashion will have changed."

"Back to '*au naturel*,' I suppose."

"*Quelle horreur!*"**

*Fr.: very stylish, fashionable, and elegant

**Fr.: How horrible!

Uncommon Tern (*Sterna rara piscator*)

"Tessa"

Herring, haddock, and whiting–Tessa loved them for breakfast, lunch, or dinner. The thrill of swooping and diving for a belly-full usually motivated her to hunt throughout the day.

But not today. She felt so tired. Yesterday, her chicks fledged. Right now, her mate was somewhere hanging out with his pals. No, today, she would stock up at the Fish Shop. She called and left her order.

On the way to the shop, she met some folks she knew. After a short conversation with a gull friend and a summer in-tern, she picked up a few essentials at the Nesting Nook. When she reached the Fish Shop, she froze at the sight of a sign hanging on the door. It read, "No, U, Tern." She puzzled over its meaning. Was the fish sold out? Were terns no longer welcome? She entered the shop and, when it was her turn, Tessa asked Morrie the counterman about the sign.

"What sign?" he asked. Tessa and Morrie stepped outside. "Beats me, Tessa. I think someone wanted the herring and haddock you ordered. And they forgot the 't' in 'not,' and what's with that comma? Say, did Gladys Gull know you were coming by?"

Tessa thought about her early morning activities and remembered her conversation with Gladys (who always did have spelling issues). "Morrie, I chatted with her this morning. I told her how weary I was and that . . ."

"That you were picking up some fish here. Well, you're a good customer and need not worry. I set your order aside. If Gladys wants herring, she'll have to place her own order." Morrie yanked the sign off the door and tore it into pieces. "C'mon in, Tessa. Your order is ready to go."

"That's a relief," she said, "Now I can get some rest."

Uncommon Tern (*Sterna rara*)

"Travis"

A Costume Ball

His best friend invited Travis to a costume ball, but Travis had no time to make a costume. To feed his diet of herring, cod, and smelt, he had to swoop and dive into the sea all day.

Travis's neighbor, Sylvester Squirrel, was standing in the sea grass next to an enormous pumpkin. He had heard Travis whining about a costume and called him over.

"Travis, I ate all the insides of this orange thing. It is hollow now, and you just might fit inside it. Would that work as a costume?"

Travis inspected the gourd. "It's a pumpkin, Sly. Nice idea, thank you, but it doesn't have enough holes for my head and both legs."

Sylvester gnawed another hole in the base and widened one near the stem. "Try it now."

After leaping on top of the pumpkin, Travis slid both his legs and then his body into the hollow gourd. Out popped his legs. "This is great, Sly. What a good costume. Only problem now is how to use it, then get out of it after the party."

"Right." Sylvester thought for a few moments. "Just roll over to the pier. Easy-peasy. When the party is over knock on my tree. I'll gnaw the shell until you're free."

Travis rolled away to the other end of the beach where waves were drumming a pier. He could hear tern friends dancing to the rhythm. As he rolled, Travis's head and legs knocked against stones dotting the sand. The pain was too much, and he cried out with every bump.

Not knowing that the howling orange sphere was their friend, the dancing terns all screeched, "Monster, monster!" and flew up in disarray.

"Hey, it's just me, Travis," he called, but even his host had fled. Travis rolled back to Sylvester.

"Back already?"

"Yup. Please gnaw me out of here. The party's over. Anyway, I need to get some dinner."

Sylvester set to gnawing. Freed from his pumpkin, Travis rubbed his bruises, flapped his wings, and flew out to sea.

Minor Marvelbird (*Avis admirari*)

"Milton"

That late afternoon, he was out on a limb again. No rescues, no cries for help, and no muggings to deter for the last four hours. Milton the minor marvelbird felt useless. An unemployed superhero bird. "I have to leave this branch office of mine. I need action, not reaction."

Milton spied a crowd at the end of his block. He flew along the rooftops until he reached the intersection of Apple and Orchard Streets. There he saw people screaming at each other, and some of them were threatening others with sticks and rocks.

"I, Milton the minor marvelbird, am here to save the day–but I will need backup." He chirped a set of trills until a host of other caped marvelbirds appeared and fluttered around his gutter pipe perch.

"What's up, Milton?" they asked in a chorus of tweets.

"That mob down there looks dangerous, my friends. Shall we break it up before anyone gets hurt?"

A cacophony of tweets, buzzes, and trills answered him.

"Then it is peck and deter time. Let's go!"

A cloud of birds descended on the mob. They pecked at ears and noses, on bald pates and hairy heads. At first, people swatted at the birds, but the pecking grew harder. At last, forgetting their quarrel, people left the intersection and scattered in all directions.

Milton gathered the flock on a nearby flat roof. "Another job well done, marvelbirds. Thank you for your help, but–" He paused. A young marvelbird lay motionless on the sidewalk. Milton flew to its side, next to a woman kneeling by the bird. She was Sherry Saver, the bird collision monitor, with a net and a box.

"Hey there, Milton. Good work. Don't worry about this one. He's stunned. We will make him better. Trust me." Milton nodded his thanks and, feeling good about the afternoon's work, he waved a wing at his friends and flew back to his branch. Perched comfortably, he snagged a beetle and settled in for a good supper.

Faculty Bird (*Avis academicus*)

"Tomaso"

Years of research had borne no fruit.

Tomaso was sure to get the boot.

The dean had told him not to tarry

Or he would give his post to Larry.

Without tenure, Tomaso stewed.

He thought the dean was awfully rude.

But late one night a concept bloomed

And Tomaso felt no longer doomed.

His new idea drew tons of praise

And he became the latest craze:

Favorite prof at Avian U.

Tenure at last–*merci beaucoup.**

*Fr.: Thank you very much.

Grumpy's Bird (*Avis malevolum*)

"George"

Those chicks are on my lawn again.

I told them stay away

Or else I'd call the lawmen

Who'd take them all away.

What, you have no place to play?

You're sorry but so blue?

Well, I will buy that empty lot

Where you can play "Cou-Cou."

Just leave my lawn and garden dear

Give them a chance to grow.

Enjoy the lot. Let's give a cheer

For this new *quid pro quo.**

–The chicks agreed.

*Latin: a favor or advantage granted or expected in return for something

Hatcher's Hairy Heron (*Ardea pilosa*)

"Tali"

Stars overhead are bright, but the moon is waxing

and in a few days it will be full.

Its light will flood the swamp and outshine the stars.

Tali raises her beak to the sky and begins her song of thanks.

The moon likes her creaky call.

With every full moon, new tendrils of delicate tresses push through her feathers.

When tendrils cover her neck and the top of her head,

she will be as full-grown as the moon and ready for romance.

Herons are known for their patience, wisdom, and perseverance.

Tali is smart; she knows the moon will shine its nurturing light,

and she patiently waits for good fortune that soon will be hers.

Dragon Bird (*Avis draconis*)

My egg arrived from outer space

On Earth it came to this bleak place.

30 million years have passed.

Yet I'm still here, perhaps the last.

A daily drink of water serves

To nourish me and quiet my nerves.

In everlasting solitude

I fly about and tend to brood.

I thought I'd be the last draconis

But yesterday I met life's bonus.

Another dragon bird and I

Have met and now we'll fly

Together.

Gerty Bird (*Avis gertya*)

Was that me? I had soft, shiny blue feathers. A flashy crown of plumes. Wings in shades of purple. Duck feet–or were those booties?

And yet, I could not fly. I saw my face, the same old me. Ah, because I could see me, I realized I was dreaming. A lovely dream.

Gerty loves birds. Birds love Gerty, and they flock to her. In her latest autobiographical book, *Gerty's Way*, seven of the book's many illustrations show her sweet connection with sparrows, ducks, geese, cardinals, chickens, and other, if odd, feathered friends.

Without Gerty's affection for birds of all kinds, this little book might never have been. Thank you, Gerty, for your dreams, your optimism, and your kindness. With best wishes for a world filled with kindness and light,

$$\text{THE END}$$

Lexicon

Translation of Latin Words for My Birds

A
Academicus	academic
Admirari	marvel
Agapornis	lovebird
Anser	goose
Ardea	heron
Aurea	golden
Autumnus	autumn
Avis, aves	bird, birds

B
Balatro	buffoon
Bubo	owl

C
Caeruleus	blue
Coquus	cook
Cuculus	cuckoo
Cynara	artichoke

D
Decaelis	of heaven
Draconis	of the dragon

E
Elige	choose

F
Formicafagensis	ant eater
Frigendus	to be cooled
Frigoris	of cold

G
Gallus	rooster
Gertya	Gerty
Gruis	crane

H
Hiemandi wintering

I
Indutusest dressed up
Irata angry

L
Lector reader
Lyricus of the lyre

M
Malevolum grumpy
Mus mouse

N
Nimis too

O
Ornatus adorned

P
Parum little
Passer sparrow
Perdiem by the day
Pilosus hairy
Pinguinus penguin
Piscator fisherman
Pluviophile rainlover
Pomonella apple moth pest
Pullus young chick

Q
Quae What

R
Rara uncommon

S
Sadsaquus an inept blundering being
Saltatens dancing

Scurrae	clownish (pl.)
Serus	late
Sterna	tern

T

Troglodytes	cave dweller

V

Vagus	wandering
Vermis	worm
Vespertilio	creature of the evening; bat
Viator	traveler

Author Bio

After several long careers in puppet theater and in museum and art education, Susan Bass Marcus began writing short stories in 2008. She continues as both a writer and illustrator and is a lifelong resident of the Chicago area.

Also by Susan Bass Marcus

Malevir: Dragons Return (2015)
Where Dragons Follow (2018)
The Wrong Move and Other Stories (2023)
Gerty's Way (2025)

www.ingramcontent.com/pod-product-compliance
Lightning Source LLC
Chambersburg PA
CBRC091722070526
44585CB00007B/147